Crushing the Fear of Public Speaking

Power Tips for Fearless Keynote Speaking Take You from Stage Fright to Rock-solid Confidence in 15 Minutes or Less

Mikael Hugg

Copyright © 2018 by Mikael Hugg. All Rights Reserved.

No part of this publication may be reproduced, distributed, or transmitted in any form or by any means, including photocopying, recording, or other electronic or mechanical methods, or by any information storage and retrieval system without the prior written permission of the publisher, except in the case of very brief quotations embodied in critical reviews and certain other noncommercial uses permitted by copyright law.

To accompany the book, we've compiled downloadable checklists, extra chapters, and bonus video content. Get these for free at:
www.mikaelhugg.com/publicspeakingbonus

*Dedicated to my wife Maria.
You believed in me even when I didn't.*

Table of Contents

Endorsements..6
Foreword by the author.........................11

Part I Motivation, Mindset, and Overcoming Fear...16

Chapter 1 – How I overcame my fears and how you can, too..17
   The moment it hit me..........................18
   Spreading the word..............................21

Chapter 2 – Why becoming a great public speaker is so important in today's economy..23

Chapter 3 – Breaking public speaking fears with the "rockstar approach"...................26
   Why we need to be in a "rockstar mode" to crush fears..28
   How I step into my "rockstar speaker persona"..28
   Finding and defining your rockstar speaker persona..29

Chapter 4 – Tackling the excuses: How to bust some common myths that hold you back from succeeding in public speaking 32
   The vicious cycle of wrong empathizers 33
   Myth 1: "You should picture the audience naked to feel more relaxed"..33
   Myth 2: "Great speakers can speak spontaneously whenever asked to do so" 35

Myth 3: "I'm not professional enough to speak in public" 37

Part II Rockstar Content Creation: How to Have Something to Deliver as a Public Speaker..**40**

Chapter 5 – When is your speech successful?..**41**
The ultimate goal of any speech is to change lives...41
Example: My speech on "How to lead millennials"..44

Chapter 6 – Know your audience, but don't dilute your message **46**
Rockstars don't sing to a different tune based on their audience..................46

Chapter 7 – Focus on just one idea **49**
Learning from great speeches....................49
Finding your governing idea helps you cut out the fluff..50
Example: How I approach my keynotes on B2B sales...51

Chapter 8 – Tell stories to tap the "campfire listener" **53**
Crafting and choosing stories to suit your speech 54
Example: My Big Fat Banker Story..........55
How to use such a story in your speech 56
Practice makes perfect................................58

Chapter 9 – Three neurochemicals triggered by great speeches **60**
Add excitement to trigger dopamine 60

  Oxytocin facilitates trust and bonding .61
  Making it fun triggers endorphin 64

Part III Rockstar Speech Delivery: Winning on Stage Every Time 65

Chapter 10 – Preparing your voice, body, and energy level 66
  Having rockstar energy 66
  Simple exercises to build up your energy level 67
  Why we need to prepare our voice 68
  My number one voice preparation exercise 69

Chapter 11 – Dos and don'ts of an excellent delivery 72
  Unnecessary explanations or apologies need to go 72
  No notes, please 73
  Finding the lost track 74
  No self-promotion if it's not a sales presentation 75
  If it isn't a lecture, don't ask questions . 76

Chapter 12 – Taking your "rockstar speaker persona" to the next level 78
  Let other people know of this book 80
  Special Thanks 81
  Social Media 83

Endorsements

"*Crushing the Fear of Public Speaking* is very engaging and easy to read, providing lots of helpful tips and myth-busters. The writing flows well and it feels as if a friend is talking to me. The content is great, too, and succeeds in covering everything needed for a book of this length."

- Dr. Emee V. Estacio, Ph.D., #1 best-selling author of *The Imposter Syndrome Remedy*, a chartered psychologist with over 18 years' experience in research

"This book is written in a casual tone that is easily relatable. The author has a knack for public speaking and inspiring others, it's infectious! This book not only covers on practical tips but also emphasizes on subtle yet important aspects of public speaking (not commonly known) like Mindset, Preparation, being in the high-performance zone and what really triggers the audience. On the practical side, I gained new perspectives like having a focus or a governing idea, curating stories around it, preparing your voice and maintaining energy levels. If you are getting started with public speaking or you are a pro this book will give you immense value."

- Emmanuel Raj, engineer, entrepreneur, investor, and finalist in the Nordic Business Forum speaker contest 2018

"This is a very well written and easy-to-read book. Like the title says it focuses on how to "crush your fear of public speaking." The book covers the subject thoroughly. It is written in a casual tone that is easy to relate to. Some of the concepts introduced in the book can also be used in other forms of communication, such as writing. It is a quick read, so I would recommend you to first read it once to get the idea, and then go through it again the day before you have to do a presentation, or a speech, to get your confidence up. Kind of wish this would have been available when I was in high school! Highly recommend this book!"

- Vesa Turpeinen, corporate business jet pilot, author, blogger, and founder of funkypilot.com

"I've previously read books on mastering public speaking, facing your fear of public speaking etc. However, none compares to Mikael Hugg's *Crushing the Fear of Public Speaking*. The chapters are easily digestible, the conversational style of writing is relatable, the examples and how-tos were clearly communicated which makes understanding the book's core concepts that much easier. I give this book five thumbs up. It's a must-read for anyone considering any career which involves speaking."

- Jenille Diaz

"As an introvert who's pretty much deathly afraid of talking to strangers on the phone, let alone doing a presentation in front of them, I really wish this book were available when I had to take that dreaded speech class way back in college! This book takes out the spook factor in public speaking. It's short, sweet, to the point, yet detailed at the same time. I started to get more into neuroscience last year, so I appreciate Mikael's discussion on neurochemicals as they relate to public speaking. I also totally resonate with his rock star analogy, and I love the flow and clarity of the book."

- Nancee-Laetitia Marin, writer, editor, and musician, thelanguageagent.com

"In *Crushing the Fear of Public Speaking*, the author tackles head on the fears that intimidate beginner public speakers. This enjoyable book is different from your typical public speaking course or book, as it provides candid, friendly advice designed to make the reader feel comfortable and at ease in front of an audience. This is exactly the kind of material I would have liked to have when I trained for public speaking and all the courses focused exclusively on the technical aspects. A must-read if you want to jump-start your career!"

- Sonia Frontera, author of *The Sister's Guides to Empowered Living*

"Though skeptical at first, the book *Crushing the Fear of Public Speaking* got much better towards the end. After a few days of reading, I concluded that definitely, this book lived up to its title. It made several valuable and helpful points, for example, about focusing on just one idea, forming an emotional connection with the audience, and enforcing the thought that the world – our perception of reality – is made up of stories. On the practical side, I enjoyed especially the exercise on how to prepare one's tongue before the speech. For me, the book reinforced practices that help in crushing fears related to public speaking, as well as introduced new and helpful ideas. I believe this book is a source of inspiration to many aspiring public speakers – especially those who have any anxiety or fear of performing in public or speaking on stage. It's not a textbook of public speaking and does not claim to be one. It offers a helping hand to take the next step."

- Karri Liikkanen, 2018 finalist in "Talk the Talk", a keynote speaking competition, author, actor, and audiovisual entrepreneur

"For anyone considering taking an offer to speak at a public event and is scared out of their minds, this book is a great place to start! Short and to the point, he offers a handful of wonderfully charming anecdotes and ideas to inspire you to give it your best. We can all be our own worst enemy when it comes to speaking in front of a group, but this book can help you push that behind you and step onto the stage with confidence!"

- Michelle Huelle

"This is an awesome book! Its straight to the point and very easy to read. Mikael highlights all the main points of public speaking and how to overcome barriers that stand in the way. He uses relevant and interesting stories to help solidify the points being made. I love his "Rockstar" approach. It's great that he also addresses some of the incorrect teachings and myths on the subject of public speaking. I definitely recommend this book to all those wanting to get improve their public speaking and take it to a "Rockstar" level."

- Jason Dansie, co-founder of Good Call

Foreword by the author

Fear is an awful thing. It stifles creativity and stops people from reaching their full potential. Therefore, learning to crush your fears is such an important skill.

The fear of public speaking often ranks highest on the list of most common phobias. According to the Statistic Brain Research Institute, 3 out 4 people suffer from speaking anxiety.

For me, the fear of public speaking was the first phobia I conquered. As I'll share later in the book, I wasn't born a public speaker. But I had the dream of becoming one.

This book will show you simple strategies that help you understand, tame, and completely crush your fears related to public speaking. If you combine the insights from all the chapters, in as short a time as 15 minutes you can go from stage fright to rock-solid confidence whenever you speak in public.

Learning to conquer your fears is the key that can take you to uncommon accomplishments. What do I mean by this?

Well, personally, I've seen the value of crushing my fears in other areas. Let me share some recent examples:

Just this year, I've crushed so many fears that had hindered me for way too long. For example, I've had a dream of writing a book about public speaking. I had started the writing process countless times but always got stuck. I blamed it most often because of the lack of time. Truthfully, it was never lack of time, per se, it was more about commitment.

Then something happened. I made a New Year's resolution that I stop being that guy who starts but never finishes, and too often listens to what his fears are saying. I decided that if I start it I'm going to commit to finishing it.

This decision changed my life. With it, I threw many old fears under the bus. Goodbye, fears!

From that day on I chose only the projects I could finish and made a clear structure for them. How many days it would take from beginning to end, what to do and when, and with whom I will do the project.

I had a master key I would use to tackle my fears: first, form a decision and then, act on it. Idleness is a breeding ground for fears. Therefore, I took my old fears head-on with decisive action.

I took on many projects that had seemed daunting or out of my league before. Disregarding old fears, I decided to go forward.

One project was to build my first American BBQ smoker and grill from scratch. I didn't have any of the necessary skills to do it but my attitude of "how hard it can be" helped me to overcome this challenge.

I went to YouTube, typed "How to build an American smoker and grill," watched tutorials, typed "how to weld," etc. It took me two weekends to finish that grill. I was super excited. (It didn't matter that I burned my shirt in the process.) I started, and I finished. Yay! So, then what next?

I realized I wanted to build a motorcycle. So, just like with the grill project, I started it, watched tutorials about how to build a motorcycle and then after five days of hard work, I had my first custom motorbike. Nice!

Here is a curious fact: Because I was determined to build that motorcycle, I attracted just the right kind of help. As a "rookie mechanic," I was mentored by a top motorcycle mechanic ... free of charge. Most likely, you would not know him by name but see his face in Grand Prix motorcycle races. With his help, I cut my learning curve from months to days!

This momentum has only grown since then. This year, I have realized more of my dreams than ever before. I love it!

With that momentum, I also decided to finish my book. Even though I had unpleasant memories from having started and quit earlier, now things were different. I had a different state of mind.

"I will write that damn book," I said to myself.

With that decision and determination, I attracted the right kind of help. My good friend and colleague, Sakari Turunen, was just the right person to help me clarify my message, and mentor every step of the way in the execution.

As for the format of the book, I decided to write a short book that is filled with hands-on information and practical tips. I believe this is the best way to write to my generation, the millennials, and actually, it works like a charm to people of all ages.

For most people, you can complete it in an hour ... or maximum two hours, if you factor in doing all the exercises. That is something anyone can do in one evening or through the course of a weekend.

I believe this is a book you can revisit often. The tips I'm sharing are something you can learn in less than an hour, but you master them by applying them repeatedly over time. Therefore, you can revisit this book many times.

Here is something crazy I still want to add, just to spark your belief that anything is possible when you are determined. When I started writing, I decided to write the book in ten days.

Ten days! My friends said I was crazy, but I did the math and yes, it was doable if I just stick with the plan. Now, it is my tenth day, and these are the final paragraphs I'm adding to this book.

The point of this Foreword is to show you that it all starts with the change in mindset. That is the reason why we do public speaking. To change minds, to change our attitudes.

When we can see life in new perspectives, we tend to live our life differently. Then real change happens. You can become a grill welder or motorcycle builder, or you can become a rockstar public speaker.

But only if you want to and only if your mindset allows you. So, dear reader, if this book gives a boost to change even one reader's mindset and put him or her to an entirely new track, I consider this as a success and that my work is done. I hope you will find public speaking as fascinating as I have.

Mikael Hugg
Helsinki, October 5th, 2018

Part I
Motivation, Mindset, and Overcoming Fear

Chapter 1 – How I overcame my fears and how you can, too

"Most unlikely to ever make it as a public speaker." That is a vote I most likely would have won in my high school years.

In my teens, I was quiet and withdrawn. I would have liked to have more friends but didn't have many.

Now, how on earth could an introverted guy like me become an extroverted "rockstar" public speaker?

If someone had asked that question from me when growing up, I would have just shaken my head. "No idea. Besides, for sure that will not happen to me."

I thought I was just missing that "public speaking gene" that other, more talented people are born with. It appeared others just seemed to have it ... and I wasn't one of them.

Sure, I would daydream about being a public speaker. But I didn't think it would be realistic at all.

But things did change.

Against all odds, I grew to make it as a public speaker. Not only did it become something that I was able to do – instead it became something I loved to do.

I love going on stage. I love sharing what I have learned. I love making an audience think, laugh, and be changed for something better.

The moment it hit me

Have you ever had a dream come true? Perhaps something you had longed for and forgotten ... before it came to pass?

For me, with public speaking, the moment of realization happened at the age of 27.

Everyone changes somewhat gradually. But there are also moments when you realize that what you have become is radically different from where you started.

In some matters, the change is so big, that it is hard to even grasp once you come to think of it.

By then, many things had happened since those teenage years. I had completed my secondary studies and graduated from the university. I had started several companies – a clothing company, a marketing agency, and a millennial leadership consultancy.

Related to the last one, I was invited to give a keynote presentation at an esteemed conference.

Just as I was about to go on stage, it clicked in my mind. Yes, this was a realization of my childhood dream.

Let me take you with me to that particular day. Here is what happened:

"And next we have Mikael Hugg," the presenter's voice echoed over the audience.

Entrance music started to play, and spotlights followed me as I started to walk to the brightly lit stage. With every step I took, I could see a sea of an audience in the dark auditorium.

Though I could not see all of their faces, I knew there were over 500 corporate leaders from all over the world. All of the participants had paid hundreds of euros to attend this event.

Behind my back, I could see the big screens showing my face and the topic.

As I climbed the stairs leading to the stage, music was still playing in the background and I could feel how adrenaline started to flow in my veins.

Then, the music stopped and for a few seconds, it felt like time had seized up. I stared at the audience and they stared at me. All the stage lights almost blinded me and for a moment I felt like I was in the center of something you would only see in the movies.

Before my turn to speak, 30 other speakers had graced the stage. But now all eyes and ears were focused on me because I was one of the two keynote speakers taking the stage.

I started my keynote with the words, "When I was a kid, I wanted to be …"

And at that moment it hit me. This was a realization of many of my childhood dreams.

In my youth, all this would have sounded like a hopeless dream. "Sure, it would be nice, but for sure it is not going to happen."

Yet, here I was. I hadn't tricked my way here. I hadn't handcuffed the actual keynote speaker and taken their turn.

No, they had invited me. They wanted to hear from me. They paid me to come – and not just with free drinks or Monopoly money, but actual Euros. Better still, they loved what I had to offer.

The speech ended with a standing ovation. Remembering my teenage self, I knew I had just gotten a significant breakthrough.

I now knew what the steps were to take that shy, withdrawn, and quiet boy and make him a rockstar public speaker.

Spreading the word

At that time, I was so happy for my breakthrough. Being confident and natural on stage was something I had aspired to be, and now I had gotten there.

In the next few years, I started sharing some of my insights both with other speakers and also those who aspired to become public speakers themselves.

Later on, I started taking on a few private coaching clients, as well. With them, I started taking what I had learned and developing a system based on these.

As I saw these strategies working for other people, I knew there would be so many more who would benefit from my thoughts and who would become better in front of others.

I mean, once you hear from three different aspiring public speakers, that they all have the same issue, same fear, or same "whatever," you know they are not alone with their questions.

Most likely, many of their questions ring a bell with you, too.

Now, I'm not going to pretend this to be a "public speaking textbook." It is a book that both goes through some relevant events in my learning path, simple strategies and "hacks" that helped me and my students, and very straight-forward ways of doing things.

I'm not going after theory but presenting something that works in real life.

I believe this book will inspire you to develop your public speaking skills. I'd love to hear more from you, so be sure to look me up on social media and let me know your thoughts.

The easiest way for this is just to join our *Facebook community "Rockstar Public Speaking."*[1] There my students and I are connecting with people who want to grow in public speaking skills. Also, it's a platform to share examples of extraordinary keynotes online.

Now, let's continue to the beef: Why is public speaking so crucial in the modern world?

---

[1] *https://www.facebook.com/groups/316536942473106/*

Chapter 2 – Why becoming a great public speaker is so important in today's economy

If you are reading this book, I believe you want to become a better public speaker.

That is a worthy goal. That is something everyone should strive to do in today's world.

The success of everything we do comes down to successful communication. This emphasizes, how vital a skill public speaking is.

It's a mighty thing. If you are successful at it, you can change someone's life on a daily basis.

I have good news for you: Public speaking is a skill we can develop and become good at.

No one is born a great public speaker. I mean, you don't even know words – let alone being able to spell them!

We as humans learn to speak through time and practice, both privately and publicly. Most people have more experience in speaking privately – to a handful of people, in an informal setting, such as a dialogue over coffee.

Those conversations only come easily if you've had practice with them. The same goes for public speaking, too. With practice, you become better, more skillful, and can make it look effortless.

In the age of social media, the importance of public speaking has grown to a new height. Digitalization is putting this on steroids because, in a more significant way than before, public speaking skills are needed to present well on video and audio.

If you think about it, in a sense, everyone is a "media source" these days. Because of the Internet and especially social media, everyone's public appearances will be easily circulated online.

Presenting your thoughts and ideas well is a crucial skill in every profession. In a sense, we are always selling our ideas to others. Sales and public speaking are so closely related that success in one usually leads to success in the other, too.

And it is not just with work. We see it's benefits in our relationships, at home, in hobbies – in every area of our lives, because everything we do is dependent on our success with communication.

Getting your point across. That is what everyone needs to succeed in.

If you think of it, great ideas are not received if they are not presented well. Good ideas that are presented well always do better than great ideas hidden in a bad presentation. Even great ideas need to be sold well.

If you want to succeed in the business world as a public speaker, I want to give you one motivating thought.

Events feature public speakers for a reason. Some people think, that speakers are just sharing data and knowledge.

But public speakers are hired because they are entertainers. They bring value to your thought processes. In your speech, you are an entertainer.

You as a person bring something more than what you could with just words and pictures.

I sincerely hope this book will not only guide you to crush all your fears related to public speaking but also get you on a track to snowball in your skill. The world is waiting for great public speakers to appear, and you could be one of them.

Chapter 3 – Breaking public speaking fears with the "rockstar approach"

Look, everyone gets afraid about public speaking at times. There isn't a single public speaker that would never be afraid.

Therefore, everyone needs to learn to crush their fears. In fact, you don't just crush them once early on in their career, but every day.

This is the key to success: You <u>don't let fear stop you</u>.

It's like riding a bike.

At first, you get confused because of pedals, chains, and steering. In the beginning, you fall many times. It feels frustrating and thoughts like "I'm not cut out for this" or "Can I just scream!" start flooding your mind.

But then one day you hop on, put your feet on the pedals and you make your first meter or two. You most likely fall after those few meters, but you feel excited. You actually rode. Then you try it again. And again. Until one day you make wheelies and jump from the cliffs.

That as an example is old, but at the same time gold. No one is born to ride a bike like a pro. Even Lance Armstrong, the professional racing cyclist, had to learn it from scratch. Most of the overnight successes take 20 years or so.

Nothing good comes easy and without practice.

Same goes with public speaking: With practice and experience, you learn to handle any undesired feelings related to making a public appearance.

But what is that fear we are talking about?

There are many feelings and emotions we could label as "fear of public speaking." A lot is going on in your guts and head when you prepare for a speech or are standing on a stage.

In a sense, you can differentiate between a "general fear of public speaking" that is related to just the thought of public speaking. Then secondly, there is "stage fright."

And I believe that becoming a rockstar is the easiest and fastest way to crush both fears. Let me explain what I mean by this.

Why we need to be in a "rockstar mode" to crush fears

No one is a rockstar when they are at home. But when a rockstar goes on stage, he or she experiences a change of mindset.

Some way or another he or she turns on the rockstar mode and ignites themselves to be ready for work.

In the rockstar you, there are no fears. When you change from the "casual you" to the "rockstar you," you abandon all your fears. You leave them in the "casual you" domain.

There are many ways to transition from the "casual you" to the "rockstar you."

For example, physical exercises, breathing exercises, and affirmations. Here is an example how I do it.

How I step into my "rockstar speaker persona"

I take 15-30 minutes to change from "casual me" to my rockstar version. During that time, everything in me changes.

I'll give some of these right away and later I will go into detail about the ones that are most helpful to you.

I have some special songs that I listen to. I like to observe the audience beforehand, if possible.

Sure, I go through many emotions. I have butterflies in my stomach and cold sweat is something that is just something I go through. It doesn't scare me. It's part of the process.

I say to myself, "I've already signed up. I get paid for this. People have paid to come to listen to me. Man up and get into your rockstar mode."

Then I start physically behaving like a rockstar. I have a posture of a rockstar, walking like one.

No, I'm not destroying every TV set in sight, but walk out that rockstar speaker persona. By this I mean I take charge of my emotions, almost like creating an alter ego that is a better version of me.

When I do the shift, the way I think and act changes.

Finding and defining your rockstar speaker persona

You really should define your "rockstar you" version for yourself. How does the person look, talk, walk, and behave?

Again, I'm not talking about a fictitious character. For the vast majority, it is not about putting on more makeup or finding just the right scarf for your persona.

But you need to have a clear picture of what that "public speaking persona" of yours looks, sounds and feels like.

If you think of Steve Jobs, he has his black turtleneck. If you think of many of the presidents, they have their trademark color tie. For any of the TV preachers, it is the tailor-made suit.

Or if you think of Steven Tyler from Aerosmith, it's everything from the long hair, no shirt but just a vest, multiple scarves and jewelry, pants as tight as possible, and so on.

Mostly, it is not about the outfit, but that can help, for sure. It is more about the inner mindset. These influence and emphasize one another so you should include both.

Take five or ten minutes now to get some clarity on your rockstar speaker persona. Start by writing this out for yourself and then actually go stand in front of the mirror to walk your persona out.

Get clear and define for yourself what you are like as a "rockstar speaker." Get it written down and etched in your body and that picture you have of yourself through the mirror.

When you are experimenting with this by yourself, you should go overboard. Be crazy – in a "you" kind of a way.

The second exercise you should do later on today, is to take some time to talk with at least three people who have heard you speak publicly. Get feedback from them, what you are like at your best.

Then, if their comments resonate with you, incorporate what they said into your rockstar speaker persona.

If, on the other hand, you don't like what you hear from them, decide to leave that version of you in the past. From now on, you define for yourself who you are on stage.

In the coming chapters, I'm going to take up different topics that help you craft your persona better. You can come back and refine your persona based on ideas that you gather.

You don't have to incorporate everything. Instead, read the coming chapters as inspiration. Take for yourself what works.

Chapter 4 – Tackling the excuses: How to bust some common myths that hold you back from succeeding in public speaking

There are many common explanations for why people are fearful of public speaking. I would call them just "myths," since there isn't any rational reason to be fearful of public speaking. All such "reasons" are just make-believe.

I'm going to be blunt here. If you think you have a good reason to be fearful of public speaking, you're wrong. Whatever your reason is, it is not valid. Sorry. You'll be a great public speaker even with (or without) that reason.

I don't want to hurt you or be rude. But I don't want you to believe any lies either. Before I go into detail about some myths, let me just say that all of these are just that: myths. They are not real. They may feel real to you, but in reality, they are not.

These are called myths for a reason. When people justify any fears, they start to think they are "*justified* fears." Then they allow the fear to take over ... because they think there is no alternative.

I'll cover in this chapter several such fears. This is not a comprehensive list, but I believe this will help you see such limiting thoughts or feelings just as that: limiting thoughts.

The good news is that you can choose to think and feel differently in the future.

The vicious cycle of wrong empathizers

Many times, people, who fear something, look for "unhelpful help." What do I mean? Well, they usually find people around them who just empathize with them in a way that helps the person still keep those fears. Therefore, they end up in a worse state, thinking that the fear they had is justified.

(If you have such friends, don't go to them for help in the future! Ask help from people who actually help you get rid of the problem ... and not just paint it pretty!)

Myth 1: "You should picture the audience naked to feel more relaxed"

I know this is something people see in a movie or have read on the internet so many times that they think it must be a fact.

Let me help you a bit here. Don't get your facts from movies or random web articles. You'll thank me later.

I don't know who initiated this idea of picturing the audience naked. Most likely someone played an April Fools prank on someone and it went viral.

If you think of speaking in public, then picturing the audience might help you relax as it may break an anxious state. However, picturing the audience naked most likely just strengthens your fear. It also distracts your attention from speaking to observing audience.

So here is what I'd advise you to do instead. If you get fearful, have a panic attack, or just lose your poise, then take a moment to compose yourself.

Breath in and out for a while. Through your nose and out from your mouth. Take your time. Look as if you were looking through the audience toward the back wall.

For some people, when a panic attack strikes, it also helps that they turn their thoughts from the audience to the fact that they are here to talk to only one, fictitious person.

Sometimes, when I have a hard time taking control of my anxiety, I try to find one person from the crowd that is giving positive signs like smiling, nodding or writing notes from my speech. After I find that one person, I kind of keep talking to that one until I get my energy and self-confidence back.

Once you are ready, then continue. The audience can't know what is going on inside of your head, so they'll think that it is just part of the show. You are in charge of the show and therefore you decide how it continues.

Remember that, you rockstar you.

Let me add one more thing. Actual rockstars forget lyrics at times. What do they do then? Well, some just point the microphone at the audience and ask them to sing!

Everything you do is part of the show. Even when you are quiet.

But only picture the audience naked if it helps you in some weird way. Otherwise, resort to the more straightforward tips I gave.

Myth 2: "Great speakers can speak spontaneously whenever asked to do so"

Many people when they see someone speak well publicly tend to think that "they have a gift," or "they were born that way" and even that "I could never be like that." None of these are true.

Sure, someone can be more gifted in something compared to someone else. But greatness does not come from giftedness but putting in the hours. Great speakers are great because they've put a lot of practice into what they do.

Let me give some examples:

If you hear someone give a great lecture, most likely they've given lectures before. Most likely they've given that very same lecture many times and have grown to deliver it well. It is a well-rehearsed act.

If you hear someone answer questions well in a public interview, most likely they were prepared to answer those questions before. Most likely they've heard the same questions or similar ones before and are therefore ready to give a well-rehearsed answer.

Or, as an analogy, if you think of a classical concert, the musicians have rehearsed the piece for hours on end. If they are spontaneous and relaxed in their delivery, it is primarily because of those hours of practicing.

In the same way, I've never heard of a play in a theater where an actor would play a part he or she hasn't rehearsed. As an actor, you rehearse to deliver all the lines word for word.

Speaking, of course, isn't acting. There are clear differences. Sure, some speakers have their speech prepared word by word. Others have an outline or structure and have many elements they are prepared to deliver ... but may decide on what elements to use based on the interaction with the audience.

So, in short: You become a great public speaker through lots of practice. Those who appear spontaneous, have put in a lot of work to have that appearance. So should you.

Personally, having been part of TED Talks, I've seen how much practice goes into it. Every speaker must go through months of training and practice with a TED approved speech instructor to prepare for their talk. It looks effortless because they have put considerable effort into it.

Reading this book can help you, but it doesn't outdo the need to practice. Therefore, you should seek opportunities to speak in public. That is the key to becoming better.

Myth 3: "I'm not professional enough to speak in public"

As I've coached people in public speaking, many have mentioned a limiting belief about themselves. Most often it is in some form of "I'm not ready yet," or "I'm not worthy," or "Someone else would be better and more qualified."

But you should know best where you are at. Therefore, you should know that with your background, you wouldn't be any better.

Let me explain this with an analogy.

Vincent van Gogh ranks as one of the best-known painters that ever lived. He is a household name, even among those who would not be able to name any of his paintings (or who think he looked like someone who played him in a movie).

It is a known fact that van Gogh hated all of his paintings. Yes, he thought they all sucked big time.

Why was this? For him, he knew all the shortcomings and mistakes. He knew the pain and suffering that went into that painting. He knew how it could have been better. He knew what his original idea was and how the end result differed from that.

Maybe it was perfectionism. Maybe it was having high standards. No matter what Vincent thought, other people had a different view. These days, people are ready to pay millions for his art.

The same goes for public speaking. When you are selected to speak from the stage, there is a reason for that. Someone wants to hear your thoughts, ideas or opinions.

No matter what your field is, there are people who know more than you about it and there are people who know less than you. There are people who would be better speakers on the subject and there are people who would be worse speakers.

But that doesn't matter. You are the one going on the stage now. You are going to deliver the best that you have. Do it with the confidence of a rockstar, because there is no reason you should whip yourself in a frenzy as van Gogh did.

Offer what you have. Don't pretend to offer more than you have. But give boldly what you do have.

Part II
Rockstar Content Creation: How to Have Something to Deliver as a Public Speaker

Chapter 5 – When is your speech successful?

Let's start with the identity of a speaker. There are many relevant perspectives to this.

Yes, as a public speaker you share information. Yes, you are also an entertainer.

From another perspective, you present your content in a way that helps the audience members receive it.

You can do this in many ways: By having an easy-to-follow structure, focusing on one idea, making your points clearly, making your speech memorable by using analogies, metaphors, stories, as well as employing a dynamic voice, and so on.

But that is not the real goal you are after.

The ultimate goal of any speech is to change lives

Your speech is successful if at least one listener is changed by it.

This change may be a realization, an aha-moment, a new perspective to a longstanding problem, figuring out a solution, making a small (or big) adaptation in one's behaviors.

To have a change that is truly impactful, it has both a new realization and because of that a decision to take practical action steps. Without any action, it remains just "a great idea."

With this definition of success, a public speaker is never just presenting information, or just entertaining the audience.

Even though you could picture a lecturer to represent the former and an MC to picture the latter one, a public speaker needs to go further.

If you think of a rockstar, he or she never comes on stage to just to "sing their songs." Whatever happens, it needs to ignite emotions and a response in the audience.

I mean, how would a rockstar feel having cried his or her soul out on a stone-cold audience without a hint of a response? It's more fun to play a gig to gravestones – at least you are not surprised by the lack of reaction.

The rockstar wants to see "a change of state" among the members of the audience. The rockstar is not satisfied if just one or few individuals get excited, they want the whole crowd is "electrified."

For the public speaker, however, it's not just about igniting a response. For example, just having a standing ovation but no changed lives is a failure to me.

Sure, getting the standing ovation is always more beautiful than not having one. I'm always humbled and grateful for such a response.

It is something the audience rewards you with if they choose to. Therefore, it indeed is a great gift to receive.

However, if it were possible, I'd always be willing to exchange a standing ovation to have more lives changed. True impact expressed in changed lives is much more rewarding than just a handclap.

A changed life shows in a change of actions. Let's look at a few examples of this.

How does this apply to different professions or situations?

A politician speaks to change the vote of the public. A basketball coach speaks to motivate his team. A teacher speaks to educate or inspire her students. All of these expect their hearers to act.

As public speakers, they are not just a "walking and talking eBook" that replays the content. No, the content is presented in a way that sparks emotions and ignites new aha moments. This, eventually, is expressed in actions.

So, what are you after as a public speaker? What is your goal as you are speaking?

Simply put, a successful speech influences how the listeners think and live their daily lives.

Example: My speech on "How to lead millennials"

Just briefly, let me cover one personal example.

One of the topics I've spoken on extensively in the last three years is that of leading millennials.

As a brief background, there are many reasons why I came to be noted as an authority in this area.

Of course, I am a member of the millennial generation myself. Secondly, my master's thesis was related to the subject, so I came to read extensively on it and to form my view.

Based on this I not only spoke to many audiences on the subject but started to coach or "reverse mentor" several executive teams in different publicly listed companies as a member of the Millennial Board.

But I don't want to just talk about millennials just for its own sake. I want my speeches to have an impact.

In my keynotes on leading millennials, the success of the speech could be that a corporate executive realizes what they or their company needs to do differently.

It can be a change of mindset, a change of behavior, taking a new focus, or something similar. Maybe it is understanding a fundamental change of thinking between two generations, and therefore finding some former behaviors or incentives obsolete.

As a public speaker, I can't go home with my listeners and lead them by the hand. The speech itself needs to give them enough to have such a realization, form a decision, and take action.

Sometimes I challenge the audience to make such decisions and take actions, and at other times it is just implied.

Well, now that you know the goal, let's look at how to get there.

Chapter 6 – Know your audience, but don't dilute your message

Many public speaking books say, "you need to know your audience." But frankly, I couldn't agree less with this idea.

All too often it is taken to the extreme, and that risks diluting the message.

Let me explain what I mean:

Rockstars don't sing to a different tune based on their audience

The Webster dictionary defines the saying "singing a different tune" as follows: "to change the way one talks about something; to have a different opinion about something."

It talks about changing one's opinions based on the audience. That is two-faced, or people-pleasing in other words. It doesn't display integrity but only shows that the person is swayed by circumstance.

You know, rockstars never play their songs differently because there is someone special in the audience.

It's their song. They present it as it was composed. If it isn't to the audiences liking, then they will search for someone else to listen to.

The rockstar should not compromise his song based on the audience.

If it has vulgar lyrics, they don't make a cleaned-up version of the song for a younger audience.

Neither do they change the lyrics, so any slang words would be explained in conventional or everyday terms.

Or make a shortened version so the elderly would not fall asleep.

Being "you" (and nothing but you) is best for your audience, too.

In a sense, it is like a trick thing. Of course you need to know, who you are speaking to, but if you are giving a talk, like a keynote, you need to be you.

The audience needs to hear the full you, the best you, the true you. Even if some don't like that "true you," that is the only thing you have to offer.

Let's take Tony Robbins as an example. He is by far one of the most successful public speakers in the world.

At the end of the day, it doesn't matter that much if Tony Robbins were to speak to a room full of lawyers or a room full of firemen.

In both situations, the audience has come to hear and experience Tony Robbins – not so much for him to relate to their profession – but to them as individuals.

So, don't be an audience pleaser. If you do, it takes something off your presentation.

Rockstars present their song uncompromisingly to any audience. So should you.

Therefore, decide to "be you" on stage. To make it entertaining, be the "rockstar you."

Then focus on "playing your song." You are not a cover band but have your original content.

Chapter 7 – Focus on just one idea

Every speech should be focused on one key idea.

This is crucial. It's the pillar of every successful speech. It really makes or breaks your speech.

If you think of the alternative, the most common problem with not-so-good speeches is stuffing too much information in one speech.

And going overboard on content destroys the speech. Therefore, just keep it simple.

Learning from great speeches

TED Talks are widely regarded as the "gold standard of public speaking." The official TED Talks feature highly skilled public speakers that have mastered the craft.

If you want to learn how vital having "just one idea" is, I suggest you watch 10 to 20 of the most viewed TED Talks. Or browse the categories and watch the top-rated speeches on a subject that interests you.

When you watch these, you will notice many commonalities. Even though the speakers are very different in style, there is at least one thing that they all share.

What is that commonality? It is focusing on one key idea.

They all have one main thought. It's never three equal main points but have one idea that ties everything together.

If that one key idea is lacking, a speech is very rarely regarded as "a great speech."

For a great speech, there is only one key idea. Sure, there can be three points in the speech, but not three main ideas.

Finding your governing idea helps you cut out the fluff

I understood this principle only after I had studied the works of Robert McKee. He is known as the screenwriter who brought the critical advice to transform the movie "Dirty Harry" from a flop to a success.

Before the movie came out, the makers of Dirty Harry were receiving lousy feedback from test audiences and didn't know what to do. So they turned to McKee for help.

Having read the script, McKee noticed the critical flaw of the movie: there was no clear controlling idea.

McKee's remedy was simple: "Get clear on your governing idea. Then cut out everything that doesn't relate to it."

The director followed this advice, which made a blockbuster hit!

Later on, McKee went on to advise Silicon Valley startups. Many of these were floundering without having anything to show for their hype and high expectations.

Utilizing this same principle of the governing idea, McKee made the startup owners realize their most critical flaw: being focused on too many things, and not having one idea to govern the rest.

McKee's consulting clients used the concept to get clear on that one governing idea and cut out the rest. As a result, the startups turned successful.

Example: How I approach my keynotes on B2B sales

One of my businesses is a sales development agency called Supersold Helsinki. I'm the co-founder and CEO of this venture that helps companies rapidly develop their sales.

One of the ways I drive new business is to give keynotes on topics relevant to sales.

One of my keynote topics is about "How systematic, professional selling is the key to success."

That is my governing idea. I want the audience to walk away thinking, "His point is that we must do systematic, professional selling if we want to succeed."

Then, all the stories I'm sharing, all my examples and analogies, are about how success comes from systematic sales.

I might have in mind favorite stories, that are funny but don't add to or relate to the governing idea.

They are superfluous. They are fluff. Therefore they need to be cut out.

When you have your governing idea, you can "kill your darlings" – your pet elements of a speech that don't relate to the main idea.

Chapter 8 – Tell stories to tap the "campfire listener"

Great keynote speeches make use of stories. Telling stories is something that works for listeners of all ages.

There is something very primitive in us as humans that stories tap. I use "primitive" here in the most positive sense of the word, meaning "deep," or "archetypal," or "essential to our makeup as human beings."

In many religions you'll find many of the key figures were great storytellers.

When Jesus taught he always used stories to help people understand more complex ideas.

Stories allow for us to take abstract concepts and explain them in every day terms, through analogy, or in ways the listeners find familiar.

Humans like to listen to stories and like to repeat them, too. Presenting information in story-form makes it easier to remember and therefore to repeat.

I would say that is how civilization started: with people telling stories. Stories allowed people to share concepts and ideas in a way that connected with the listener. As a result, reality as we perceive it, is the sum total of the stories we've heard and passed on.

Crafting and choosing stories to suit your speech

Good stories have a beginning, a middle and an end. When you hear a story for the first time, you don't know the end from the beginning.

When you speak more, you find that you have several main stories that you tell often. These are stories you are very familiar with, that you know to work, and that you can present well to any audience.

You can share personal stories to simultaneously get two different kinds of results. First, to share something relevant to your governing idea. Second, to share something about you – which can make you, for example, more trustworthy or likable to the audience.

With stories, you can change the mood of the audience and spark emotions. Therefore, you should have several stories in your speaker toolbox, so you can use them when you see a need.

Here is one story I tell quite often:

Example: My Big Fat Banker Story

From early childhood I always wanted to be a banker.

In the daycare or at the primary school, all the other kids said they wanted to become firemen or policemen. But when the teachers asked me about my future dreams, I wanted to be a businessman or a banker.

Go ahead, picture a 5-year old in a pinstripe suit. That was my dream!

In my teens, I still had the same goal. I started reading business papers, such as Forbes or The Financial Times. Living in Finland, these were not something available on the local newsstands, so my father subscribed to the paper and had it airmailed from the US.

At that time, I saw being business literate crucial for my future success. I needed to invest much time and effort in these preparatory years before my great banker dream would manifest as reality.

I thought reading up on the financial news would prepare me for adulthood and the profession of a banker. Therefore, I continued for years to subscribe to these papers.

For my senior year in high school, I went to study in an international school in Luxembourg. My hunger to become a banker was burning hot in me.

At the end of the year, having just turned 18 years old, I applied to work in one of the biggest international banks in the world.

Then I got the news: I was accepted! My dreams had become a reality. Having just passed adolescence, I started working in the Luxembourg branch office of this giant of a bank.

I was living my dream. I would have been happy to start working for any local bank or national bank, but here I was in the epicenter of the banking industry.

My work was in the private wealth management department. If you know anything about the world of banking, this was the best growing bed for an aspiring banker.

But then all of a sudden, after three months, I quit my job. I walked out and decided never ever to work in the banking industry again.

How to use such a story in your speech

Having heard that story, the audience has many questions popping up in their mind.

"So, what had happened? Was it his fault? Was he not cut for it? Or did the corporation do something wrong? Did the company not nurture us as employees that I decided never to work there?"

The story leads listeners to understand the point you want to make. Therefore, the same story can be used for many different goals.

Based on the governing idea of the speech, I may tell that story in slightly different ways. Depending on the point I'm wanting to make, I emphasize different parts of the same story.

If the topic is leadership, I focus on those aspects. If it is building your personal career, I'll shift my focus accordingly.

It is not necessary or even helpful to tell everything about your story. You cut out the parts that don't relate to your governing idea.

I always work my way backward. First, I think, what point do I want to make. Then I come up with a story to make that point and starting from the conclusion I go through how the story is made up and how it begins.

What are your stories? Everyone has such personal anecdotes from their life that can be a source of a great story.

You can turn everyday events into stories. Your day to day life can be a great source of stories.

Practice makes perfect

You should always practice your stories a lot. Preferably, do this to a live audience of at least one person.

I usually practice a story tens of times to get it right. Sometimes I take hundreds of times to practice the story in depth.

I do most of my practicing with my wife – either at the office, at home or taking a long walk outside. It can be a friend, a colleague, or someone else who wants to develop their public speaking skills.

Look up your local toastmaster for a peer group or join our *Facebook community "Rockstar Public Speaking"*[2] to find like-minded individuals from all around the world.

Other people can help you to develop and fine-tune your stories. At times, you may be oblivious that what you are sharing is hitting home with a listener. With their feedback, you can make the story even better.

Many of the stories in this book are mine, but they've found their final form only through working

---

[2] https://www.facebook.com/groups/316536942473106/

with other people. I have certain key people that give me feedback and stories.

In fact, some of the stories that I share here were first coined and crafted by my content strategist. He knew what had happened in my life, wrote it as a story, and then after I validated it, it became part of the book.

Chapter 9 – Three neurochemicals triggered by great speeches

Let's have a brief look at the biochemistry of great speeches. Great speeches trigger chemical responses in the brain.

Three different brain chemicals are of particular interest to us: dopamine, oxytocin, and endorphin.

I'm not listing these, so you would start to take blood samples from the audience or asking them for brain scans.

But understanding what triggers them can help you craft a more impactful speech. So, I don't want to lecture you on chemistry but give a layman's version of what happens inside our brains while listening to a piece of oratory excellence.

Add excitement to trigger dopamine

In the brain, neurotransmitters are chemicals released by neurons (or nerve cells) to send signals to other nerve cells. Dopamine is one of these.

The brain includes several distinct dopamine pathways. One of these plays a significant role in how we are motivated, especially in reward-motivated behavior. Anticipating rewards increases dopamine in the brain.

Can you feel saliva already forming on your tongue? That is one great example.

Great speeches trigger dopamine for example by adding suspense which we expect to come to a conclusion.

In stories, cliffhangers bring up adrenaline. Good thriller and action movies trigger dopamine because it makes the viewer anticipate what is coming next. If you know the feeling of hanging to your seat, that is what I'm talking about.

In the singing competitions on TV, just before they go to a commercial break, they leave a cliffhanger: they tell you what will be coming after the break, so you won't change the channel.

Similarly, in speeches, you can hint at what is coming to make the audience hungry for it.

Oxytocin facilitates trust and bonding

Oxytocin is a hormone that neurons use to communicate with one another. It plays a role in social bonding, sexuality, and childbirth.

To speak in an impactful way, there has to develop a bond between the speaker and the audience. This is what makes oxytocin interesting to us.

If the audience can't trust and bond with you, they remain outsiders. Then, they are not as likely to receive the message and be impacted by it.

If you were a superhuman that became an astronaut at age 15 and graduated from several universities before you were 18, your audience might be impressed but not bonded. Most people can't relate to that experience.

Bonding comes from finding common ground and commonalities.

Personal stories, sharing not just your accomplishments and accolades but also some of your wounds make you more humane, likable, and the audience can feel a bond with you.

People don't want to share pains. But that is one of the things that will create trust and bonding. When you share something personal, and even open up your own life not holding back, the audience is taken by your openness, boldness, and willingness to share, that they reward you by bonding with you.

One speech that always comes to mind for me was that given by one great comedian. His story was about living simultaneously in two different worlds.

He was working for a late-night show, but at the same time, his two-year-old child was going through cancer.

In the daytime, the whole family was fighting cancer, trying to get it into remission mode. At the same time, he needed to be super funny in the night time.

However, the treatments were successful, and things started looking promising. Maybe there was light at the end of the tunnel.

The man was also promoted at work, so he had a more significant responsibility in the late-night show. The producers just asked that he needed to be even funnier than before.

The same day he got the news of his promotion, he also received a second message. The cancer had returned after a period of remission. To make matters worse, when cancer recurrence happens, it is always tougher the second time.

This mix was taking its toll. Under pressure, his jokes started getting darker. Things were tight in the family financially. Money was sparse because everything went to the treatments.

Even though I can't fit the whole story here, the point was this: He shared the story in a way that had the audience crying.

This caused oxytocin to flow. Everyone could feel his pain. For sure, it was a story the listeners would remember for the rest of their lives. I sure do.

Making it fun triggers endorphin

Endorphins are our very own drug with the principal goal of inhibiting pain signals and causing feelings of euphoria. The name "endorphin" has two parts: endo- which is short for "endogenous," meaning "of internal origin" and -orphin, which is shortened from "morphine." Thus, it is intended to mean "a morphine-like drug our body produces."

This is triggered in speeches by fun and humor.

For example, you might start with a humorous story. Often, it is not a joke – unless you have one related to the governing idea.

If you think of the end result of your speech, often it is to leave the audience elated feeling good feelings.

But having just rough stories and being too dramatic work toward the opposite goal.

The comedian with the child having cancer shared his story in a way that leaned heavily to the dramatic side, but it was spiced up with humor – in the midst of all the pain and suffering.

Part III
Rockstar Speech Delivery: Winning on Stage Every Time

Chapter 10 – Preparing your voice, body, and energy level

Public speaking differs from all other everyday situations. Therefore, you can't engage it in the same way as other things.

Some speakers fail to understand that voice is just a byproduct of your whole body-language. Before speaking on a stage, they only do some simple voice exercises as preparation. I think this is a grave mistake.

Sure, your voice is your number one tool in public speaking. You should be able to use it effectively.

But to get to this, you can't just do voice preparation but prepare your whole body and, on a deeper level, hike up your energy level so you are ready to perform.

This, also, is a great way to crush any fears. Having a high energy level stomps on the fears.

Having rockstar energy

Like a rockstar, you need to be ready to give your best. The audience is not waiting to see and hear the average you, but the "best you." Give them just that.

In a sense, as a speaker, you need to be hyperactive or hyper-energetic. You need to make sure you are full of energy and able to express that.

When you are giving a speech, what may seem "over the top" or "exaggeration" in ordinary life, is in fact very good.

To you, it may feel like you are going overboard with your energy. With time, you get used to that.

For many public speakers, just being in front of a live audience or cameras gives a spurt of energy. They step into a different mode.

But you can't rely on the audience or the cameras to be your only source of energy. Make sure you have prepared yourself in other ways.

Here are some ways I've found helpful to prepare before going on the stage.

Simple exercises to build up your energy level

Tony Robbins is an excellent example of a high-energy speaker. He makes everything he does on stage look natural.

Before going on stage, Tony jumps on a trampoline. For him, this is a great simple way to activate his whole body.

On the trampoline, all of your body is going up and down and getting a gentle exercise, without breaking a sweat.

For me personally, I like walking around. I either walk behind the stage or go outside. That boosts my energy nicely before going on stage.

Other speakers I know do some whole-body exercises and stretches.

What for you would be the best way to raise your energy level and prepare your whole body for performance?

Find a way to prepare yourself in a way that works for you. You need to have your whole body prepared before going on stage.

Now that you know this, we can finally take a look at how to prepare your voice.

Why we need to prepare our voice

In our normal daily life, we all tend to have our voice more monotonous and not articulate words that clearly. But when you are on stage, you can't be monotonous or inarticulate.

How does one use one's voice effectively? Well, for example by changing the volume. This means that you can speak loudly and then again softly, even whispering at times.

Also, to fight monotony, you should be able to change your pitch to higher and lower. Just think about how people vary their voice in the Spanish speaking countries and you will get the idea.

For example, when you share a story, you should change your voice to emphasize different parts and different moods of the story.

But how, then, should you prepare your voice?

Let me be clear here: You should not worry, if you have a speech impediment, or if you are speaking a second language with a funny accent.

These are just part of you. They add to your character.

Just think about Arnold Schwarzenegger: his Austrian accent hasn't done him any harm but is his trademark. In the same way, embrace those parts of you and let them be part of who you are.

Then again: Not opening up your voice with proper vocal warmup exercises just isn't professional.

My number one voice preparation exercise

Many people think that to prepare or warm up your voice, you should focus on your throat or your tongue. Sure, these are important, but they are not most important.

To pronounce well and articulate clearly, you need to prepare first and foremost your lips and your jaw. You have to wake up your jaw and lips to have clear articulation.

There are many voice preparation exercises. I've tried many of them, but there is one that stands out from the rest.

For me and many of my students, this exercise does more than all the rest combined.

Here is the formula:

1. Find a place you can be by yourself

Usually, preparation is something you favor doing alone. You don't want to have any distractions, engage in conversations, or anything like that.

With this exercise, I'm giving a heads-up that you might look goofy doing it so having privacy gives you an extra benefit.

2. Stick out your tongue as far out as you can.

You don't need to overdo it to feel a gag reflex but stick it out as far as you reasonably can.

3. With your tongue sticking out, count out loud numbers from one to twenty, actively using your jaw and lips

This sounds like "waw – too – tee" and so on, all the way to "tweety."

Now, this is the part where you might sound and look funny, but that is not a problem.

And what is the benefit of this?

Well, you can test it for yourself. Do the exercise and pay attention afterward. Do you hear the difference? You should notice especially how your S's sound. They should be much clearer now.

One final tip for those times when you can't prepare privately (and don't want to look like an idiot in front of other people), you can also do this exercise silently.

Chapter 11 – Dos and don'ts of an excellent delivery

There are many ways to ruin a good speech. I gathered here some examples that set you up to fail.

If you are prone to do any of these, make an extra effort to weed them out!

Unnecessary explanations or apologies need to go

One thing people tend to do when they go on stage is to start with an apology. This is a giveaway for who is an amateur speaker and not a professional.

"Sorry, I forgot my notes." "Sorry, I don't have a presentation." "Sorry, my mouth is dry." "Sorry, that I'm jet-lagged." "Sorry, I'm not prepared." "Sorry, I'm not as good as you are."

For the speaker, this is a natural opener. It seems casual, open, and truthful – but actually, you are just annoying the audience for no reason or benefit.

All of these just come through as "Sorry, I'm unprofessional."

If I refer back to the concept of governing idea from earlier on, if the issue you are apologizing for doesn't relate to your governing idea, then don't mention it.

If, for example, you forget your notes, the audience doesn't need to know it. You just accept the situation and make it part of your presentation.

And when it comes to notes, anyway, you should have none. Let me explain this right away.

No notes, please

It just gives you a false sense of security having your notes in front of you.

The worst thing, in my opinion, is to have a stack of papers as your notes to either refer to or to read from.

I hate seeing a politician give a speech reading from paper. I'm mesmerized by such lack of skill in public speaking.

Have you ever heard a politician give a speech reading from a paper where he or she, for example, "condemns the country for their human rights violations," and expounding "how outraged we are as a nation," and so on?

They are reading it from paper and it doesn't sound right. Their feelings are not reflected.

They are just a walking "audiobook reader."

As a profession public speaker, they should be ready to captivate the whole audience. The words should make an impression on the listeners. The words need to express your feelings not just in letter but also in tone.

So, please, don't use notes. Rehearse so well that you don't need notes.

Then, the only issue you might have is forgetting your train of thought. To help you out, I have a way around that issue, too.

Finding the lost track

With or without notes, you may lose your train of thought. This is something that can happen to anyone. Therefore, don't fret about it.

Even professionals may forget where they were and what they had planned to say next. They experience a blackout and need to find a way back.

Again, not needing to make apologies, here is a simple way how to proceed.

First of all, be ok with taking the time you need. You are in control, so you can decide how this goes.

Also, you can take a sip of water and just observe the audience. Don't even try to think about where you were at. Just relax and gain composure.

If you don't remember right away, the best way to proceed is actually to take the next topic. Do it without any explanations.

Then if you remember what you left out you can find a way to include it later in your speech.

A lot of the things that happen on stage are about self-management. Managing your feelings and thoughts leads you to become a more confident and therefore less fearful public speaker.

No self-promotion if it's not a sales presentation

A great speech is focused on what happens in that encounter. Sure, the speaker can challenge the audience to take practical steps as a result.

However, you should not sprinkle your speech with blatant self-promotion with the hidden (but plainly visible) agenda that people would buy more from you.

Of course, it helps the audience to take in what you are saying when they know who you are and where you are coming from.

For keynote speeches, there is a master of ceremony to present the speaker. Therefore, the keynote speaker does not need to present himself.

If, however, you need to present yourself, you can do it gracefully.

If it isn't a sales pitch, don't go overboard and start listing "I come from this company, this is what we do, these are our key clients."

No one cares – unless you are pitching to raise more funding. Therefore, on all other occasions, don't do it.

People are interested to hear your big idea. That is what you should focus on, instead of all your background and your company.

If it isn't a lecture, don't ask questions

This seems to be a problem for speakers that have already done some speaking gigs and are on the fast track of becoming a professional speaker.

Academics seem to have this problem as well.

Asking questions and "making the speech more interactive" is highly unpleasant for the members of the audience.

When you are a keynote speaker and talking to hundreds of people, you should concentrate on delivering a top-notch speech, not a top-notch quiz of who is in your slide's picture (even if it were obvious) or making audience shout guesses of how many bicycles are in the world.

Asking questions and then seeking one brave listener from the crowd makes the whole audience tense and awkward, and it cuts your flow.

If it isn't a lecture, stop making it one.

Instead of asking questions and making quizzes, you can always embed them into your story.

The question, "Who is in the picture," could be rephrased as "here's Einstein, a man who..."

Remember, people are there to learn about your big idea, not participating in a quiz show.

The only questions you should ask your audience are ones that only require raising their hand. For example, "Who among us is a millennial?" or "Who has seen all the seasons of 'Game of Thrones'?"

If you are asking specific numbers, names or whatever else other than yes or no questions, stay away from asking questions at all.

Chapter 12 – Taking your "rockstar speaker persona" to the next level

The goal of this book was for you to define for yourself and develop in practice your rockstar persona.

If you skipped the exercise in chapter three, go back to it now. If you did complete it earlier, take some time now to review it.

You need to have your "rockstar speaker persona" identified on paper. Write it down!

If you'd like feedback on your rockstar speaker persona, just come to our *Facebook community "Rockstar Public Speaking."* Many readers of the book are members there, especially those who want to develop their skills.

Secondly, you need to see and feel it. Therefore, go in front of a mirror, and act it out. Take a speech and perform it to an imaginary audience – as the "rockstar you."

Then practice your talk in front of a live audience. It can be just one person, but someone has to listen to you.

With their feedback, you can refine your "rockstar speaker persona."

Challenge yourself and go "all in"

Like I wrote earlier, I want to see lives changed. And that applies not just to my speeches but to the books I write.

I'm more eager to see lives changed than just tickle ears.

One of the keys that helped me grow better at public speaking was that I sought out opportunities to speak in public. Sounds simple, right?

Well, I want you to make use of everything you've learned. I've learned that the best motivation for you to learn is … if you have to!

So, why don't you go ahead and get contracted as a public speaker? I've put together a video course for you. It'll show you step by step, how you can land your first paid speaking gig, and be featured in conferences, seminars, and on TV.

I already mentioned this in the beginning of the book, but in case you missed that earlier, I want to give that offer again. Find extra materials that complement the book for free at:

www.mikaelhugg.com/publicspeakingbonus

By the way, it is free. It is my way of saying "thank you" for taking the time to go through this book.

Let other people know of this book

Thank you so much for being a finisher! You read the book until the end.

I'd like to ask you for a favor. Would you consider taking 2 minutes and writing your review on Amazon?

Just write briefly, what you liked best about the book, who you think would benefit from reading it, and if you have some ideas to make it better.

I'd love to hear your feedback "fresh off the bat" as you just went through it. With your help, I hope to make future versions of the book even better.

I have a surprise for everyone who writes me reader feedback. You can send your comments to mikael@mikaelhugg.com and I'll send you my surprise gift. (Please allow me some time to respond, as I read all of these personally.)

Special Thanks

I dedicated this book to my wife Maria, the love of my life, who has been there for me all these years. Without you, this book would still be a dream. Because of you, I am the man I am today.

Also, I want to give my special thanks to Sakari Turunen, who gave his endless support during this project and made sure that everything went smoothly. Writing a book is so much more than just typing words on paper. Truth to be told, getting the book out and available for everyone takes so much time, knowledge, and effort.

I was able to create this book in ten days, mainly because of Sakari's endless pushing and forcing, planning and execution. He is a true professional when it comes to getting things done. This world needs thousands and thousands more like you. So, once more, thank you Sakari Turunen, you are an inspiration to so many people – I included.

This book has also other supporters, pre-readers, who gave me precious comments and feedback. Here is the list of the people I definitely want to thank: *Emmanuel Raj, Rami Paramo, Stina Dansie, Jason Dansie, Karri Liikkanen, Juho Tunkelo, Lasse Rouhiainen, Pentti Mäkinen, Mirja-Liisa Mäkinen, Carlos Braz, Franz Mittler, Jaana Villanen, Saara Vehoniemi, Aleksi Lehtola, Joel Mäkinen, Lotta Salminen, and Jan Eriksson.*

Also, I want to thank <u>Gundi Gabrielle's Facebook group</u>, who gave me a lot of insight and tips for making this book happen.

The last but not least is our <u>Kindle Launch Advisors Facebook group</u>, which members helped with their participation to get cover right, words right, and so many other details, as well.

This book would not be complete if I wouldn't add a picture of our "hairy baby," dachshund puppy Napsu. Get to know him through his instagram @napsuthenapoleon.

Social Media

If you wish to follow me, check these out:

Websites:

www.supersoldhelsinki.com

www.mikaelhugg.com

www.actionmattersmost.com

Twitter:

@MikaelHugg

Linkedin:

Linkedin.com/in/mikaelhugg

YouTube:

Mikael Hugg

Email:

mikael@mikaelhugg.com

Instagram:

mikaelhugg

Made in the USA
San Bernardino, CA
26 January 2019